My Life on an Island

Cindy James

Rosen
REAL
READERS

Published in 2010 by The Rosen Publishing Group, Inc.
29 East 21st Street, New York, NY 10010

Copyright © 2010 by The Rosen Publishing Group, Inc.

Book Design: Ronald A. Churley

Photo Credits: Cover, p. 1 by Clayton Davis; p. 2 © VCG/FPG International; pp. 3, 6 © Townsend P. Dickinson/The Image Works; p. 4 © Arlene Collins/The Image Works; p. 5 © Bob Daemmrich/The Image Works; p. 7 © G. Gardner/The Image Works.

ISBN: 0-8239-8104-5
6-pack ISBN: 0-8239-8506-7

Manufactured in the United States of America

CPSIA Compliance Information: Batch #WR112190RC: For further information contact Rosen Publishing, New York, New York at 1-800-237-9932.

My Life on an Island

Cindy James

The Rosen Publishing Group, Inc.
New York

I live on an island.

I see water around my island.

I see boats near my island.

I see shells on my island.

I see birds on my island.

I can play on my island.

Words to Know

birds

boats

island

shells

water

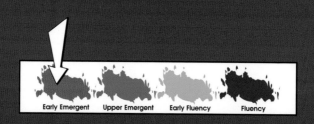

Early Emergent   Upper Emergent   Early Fluency   Fluency

The Rosen Publishing Group, Inc.

C1

9 780823 981045

ISBN: 0-8239-8104-5
6-pack ISBN: 0-8239-8506-7